MW00936258

30 Days of

STRENGTH

for

A woman's heart

Devotional by

Lisa Cook

30 Days of STRENGTH
for a woman's heart
"Connecting the heart of women with the heart of God"
By Lisa Cook

**Copyright info
February 2016,
Lisa Cook of 4 His Beloved Ministries.**

All rights reserved.
No part of this publication may reproduced, stored in retrieval systems, or transmitted, in any form or by any means, electronic, mechanical, photocopying, recording, or otherwise, without written prior permission of the author.

Unless otherwise noted, Scripture is taken from the New King James Version®. Copyright © 1982 by Thomas Nelson. Used by permission. All rights reserved.

Scripture quotations taken from the New American Standard Bible®,Copyright © 1960, 1962, 1963, 1968, 1971, 1972, 1973,1975, 1977, 1995 by The Lockman Foundation Used by permission." (www.Lockman.org)

Scripture quotations from THE MESSAGE. Copyright © by Eugene H. Peterson 1993, 1994, 1995, 1996, 2000, 2001, 2002. Used by permission of Tyndale House Publishers, Inc.

Scripture quotations marked (ESV) are from The "ESV" and "English Standard Version" are registered trademarks of Crossway. Use of either trademark requires the permission of Crossway. (ESV®), copyright © 2001 by Crossway, a publishing ministry of Good News Publishers. Used by permission. All rights reserved."

Contents

Day One – Mind Wars   5

Day Two – Pick up the Pace   7

Day Three – Keep it Real   9

Day Four – My Prosperity is His Pleasure   12

Day Five – Eye Opening Experience   14

Day Six – Do you see her   16

Day Seven – One to Another   18

Day Eight – Boldly Confident   20

Day Nine – Preparing Daily   22

Day Ten – Grandma's Faith   24

Day Eleven – My Beloved   26

Day Twelve – Cast Your Burden   29

Day Thirteen – Known by Name   31

Day Fourteen – Newborn Hunger   34

Day Fifteen – A Desolate Place   36

Day Sixteen – Chosen   39

Day Seventeen – Faith and Destiny   41

Day Eighteen – Intense Desire   43

Day Nineteen – Downcast to Up-Cast   46

Day Twenty – Ordinary to Extraordinary   48

Day Twenty One – Waiting and Wondering   51

Day Twenty Two – Living a Legacy   53

Day Twenty Three – Why Persevere   55

Day Twenty Four – Diamond in the Rough   57

Day Twenty Five – Promised Purpose   59

Day Twenty Six – As He Is   62

Day Twenty Seven – Joshua's Secret   64

Day Twenty Eight – Prepared and Ready   66

Day Twenty Nine – The BEST is still to Come   68

Day Thirty – With God   71

Mind Wars

My focused prayer for this season: To become increasingly aware of self-defeating, enemy-accusing, sister or brother-bruising thought patterns! To take them captive unto victory in Christ - swiftly!

Maybe you are like me... tired of missing out on God's best because sometimes my focus gets captivated by the worst! Let this be a year when this curse gets reversed!

Our thought life plays a tremendous role in our faith; in fact it is central to whether or not we will experience victory on a daily basis in Christ and enjoy the fuller blessings of God in our life. Our thoughts can either impede us or infuse us with vitality and life.

*"Therefore gird up
the loins of your mind,
be sober, and rest your hope
fully upon the grace
that is to be brought to you
at the revelation of Jesus Christ"
1 Peter 1:13*

"Girding up" was a practice of that time period in which an individual would take the loose ends of their long garment and tuck it into a leather belt that was wrapped around their waist. Binding it securely so that it would not impede their movements. Whether engaging in battle, setting out on a journey, or doing their daily work this would give them the freedom to move and make progress without restriction or hindrance.

When we allow our thoughts to be ruled by our carnal nature of unbelief, we impede our own progress in Christ. *Girding up the loins of our mind* requires a deliberate effort on our part to exercise some discipline, "cinching in" our thoughts with the Word of God by the power and presence of the Holy Spirit. <u>We have been given and entrusted with everything we need to live a progressive, abundant, overcoming, fruit-bearing life in Christ.</u> But we must choose to exercise faith, putting on the mind of Christ daily, a decision God will not force us to make.

So... looking ahead I choose to be more proactive in my thought life, choosing to cast off unbelief, doubt and discouragement through bold Christ-centered faith! Will you join me?

Let's pray...
Father, thank You for Your living Word and powerful presence in my life! Please help me to be more aware of my thoughts and where they tend to linger so that I can cast off unbelief and put on right thinking. Today, I choose to honor You in my thoughts! In the victorious Name of Jesus! Amen

Pick up the Pace

A few months ago, my daughter participated in a triathlon for beginners. This athletic challenge consisted of a quarter mile of swimming, ten miles of biking, and 3 three miles of running. All done in consecutive order. Even for beginners it was pretty intense. I was so proud of her! She had gone through a surgery just eight weeks prior and wasn't sure if she would make it, but she pressed through and completed all three courses. However, right after she crossed the finish line, following close on her heels was an 84-year old man. Yes, that is correct-84 years old! Later my daughter confessed, somewhat jokingly, that when the finish line was in view she could hear the man gaining on her so she pressed herself to *pick up the pace,* not wanting to be outdone by an "*old guy.*" At least she could say "I beat the *old man*" (lol).

Of course, in all seriousness, we were completely taken by this 84-year *old man.* Very few in their 50's and 60's have the agility and strength he displayed at 80. What kind of training, discipline and perseverance does it take to get your body to cooperate at that age? I was thoroughly impressed and inspired by his example. Inspired *not* to participate in triathlons but to finish *my* race well. The apostle Paul expressed the same desire:

"I don't know about you,
but I'm running hard for the finish line.
I'm giving it everything I've got.
No sloppy living for me!
I'm staying alert and in top condition.

*I'm not going to get caught napping,
telling everyone else all about it
and then missing out myself. "*
1 Corinthians 9:26-27 (The Message)

By the grace of God and the power of the Spirit, Paul did what he set his heart to do:

*"I'm about to die,
my life an offering on God's altar.
This is the only race worth running.
I've run hard right to the finish,
believed all the way.
All that's left now is the shouting-God's applause!
Depend on it, he's an honest judge.
He'll do right not only by me,
but by everyone eager for his coming."*
2 Timothy 4: 7-8 (The Message)

I also want to "*run hard right to the finish line*" inspiring others to "*pick up the pace*" as I go. Of course the prerequisite is staying alert, in top spiritual condition and giving it everything I've got. How about you? This really is the only race worthy of giving everything we've got.

Let's pray...
Father, my goal and great desire is to finish well. Help me to stay focused and alert, free from spiritual apathy. Grant me Your divine enablement to stay active and run hard so that I may inspire others to pick up the pace even as I cross the finish line. In the name of my Victor and Champion -Jesus Christ! Amen!

Keep it Real

"I woke myself up snoring last night"
Yep! You read that correctly. I woke *myself* up. (lol)

...there I said it! Just keeping it real.

Also, while I am keeping it real, my kitchen sink is currently full of dishes, my bathrooms are overdue for a cleaning and my office looks like a tornado hit. Oh, *Calgon* take me away (or *not* since the bathtub is dirty too). And since I am <u>keeping it real</u> I want to testify to my firm belief and conviction in the existence of angels. Why? Because I am certain my 3 adult children would not be alive today if it had not been for their protective involvement while they were growing up. Example: Once when my oldest son was crawling (at 8 months, *not now*) I found a fork shoved into an outlet. Baby with a fork and no outlet cover - *not a good combination*. Don't ask, but thank God for angels!

I also confess, at times I have prided myself on forgiving well, but I have discovered this is mostly because I forget well. This is great for forgiving but not so great when it comes to things like birthdays and anniversaries. Nothing like springing to the store for a last-minute gift, frustrated because you can't find anything decent, and then wondering why that person decided to be born on that day anyway. What is the point of this?

Answer:

"Then Jesus said to them,
"Take heed and beware of the leaven

of the Pharisees and the Sadducees."
And they reasoned among themselves,
saying, "It is because we have taken no bread."
Matthew 16:6-7

They thought Jesus was chiding them for their failure to remember to bring bread. They thought He was rebuking them for their forgetfulness, their humanness. Yet this was the furthest thing from His mind, the least of his concerns.

It is easier than you think to fall prey to the "leaven of the Pharisees". Painting a picture of perfection, only revealing what looks good, clean, together and tidy is a form of leaven. This kind of leaven puts a strangle hold on us and communicates a false reality to others. An impossible standard. Truth is, none of us is perfect, and to paint a picture of perfection becomes more about me than about Him and His super abundant grace.

I couldn't be perfect if my life depended on it and thankfully, because of His grace, it doesn't!

For our sake and the sake of others let's "keep it real." This gives people freedom to fail, make mistakes, forget, and at times even "flake out." Freedom for people to be who they are without the fear of rejection for who they are not. Freedom for them to enjoy His great grace through us!

I am not advocating being irresponsible or lazy, but rather seeking to release the unnecessary tension of trying to maintain a perfect appearance. Our goal is not human perfection but love from a pure heart connected to God's. He loves us in our imperfection and desires for us to rest in His perfect grace!

So let's "keep it real" and be known as people generous in grace!
"By the grace of God I am what I am..." 1 Corinthians 15:10

Let's pray...

Father, please help me to be real! To not fall into the trap of perfectionism. Your grace is my resting place and Jesus is my glory! I want to walk in grace and be gracious. In the Name of Jesus, the Author and Finisher of my salvation!

Does God want me to prosper?

"Let the Lord be magnified,
Who has pleasure in the prosperity of His servant."
Psalm   35:27b

Do you ever struggle with the concept of God taking pleasure in your personal prosperity? If the answer is yes, you are not alone. Yet the truth is everything He has ever done both in creation and redemption have been for our prosperity.

The word prosperity means to be successful, flourishing or thriving. The Hebrew word is *shalom* and is translated completeness, soundness, welfare and peace.

A close study of this word shows it has to do with the wellbeing of the entire person.

Jesus said...

"Peace I leave with you,
My peace I give to you;
not as the world gives do I give to you.
Let not your heart be troubled, neither let it be
afraid." John 14:27

What kind of peace does the world give? The kind that is conditioned upon instability. But God gives us peace and prosperity based on the finished work of Christ! A work that cannot be altered or corrupted.

The Lord not only takes pleasure in our peace and prosperity but has provided a secure means for us to be at peace and prosper.

We need to let our minds soak in this truth. Life can be hard, but God is good and only seeks our best and highest good! As we trust in and rely upon Him we should expect good, not evil. We should look for triumph not fear tragedy. We should anticipate His favor, not a fearful expectation of judgment! We should be confident knowing He is for us and not against us!

> ## "Do not fear, little flock,
> ## for it is your Father's good pleasure
> ## to give you the kingdom."
> ## Luke 12:32

And what a glorious Kingdom it is! Complete with privileges and blessings beyond compare. I encourage you to write this down: "God takes pleasure in *my* peace and prosperity therefore good things are prepared for my future!" Then begin the next 30 days by declaring this statement to bring your heart and mind into practical alignment with the Truth: God is good!

Let's pray...
Father, I celebrate that everything You are involved with prospers. Your nature is to bless! You can only give good gifts! So I look to the future and laugh at the days to come because of who You are and my relationship with You through Christ. In the Name of Jesus my Redeemer! Amen!

I made a quick run to the store today to pick up a couple of greeting cards. This particular store had a limited selection. After perusing the aisle, a couple of times over, it was beginning to look as if I may need to drive somewhere else. I felt pressed for time so I paused and asked the Lord, *"Please* show me if there are any cards I am overlooking that are suited for this need". Before I finished the prayer, my eyes rested upon the category for which I had been searching. Some would say it's a coincidence but I don't, not for a moment! This is a very small example of how the Lord desires to "open our eyes" to things we can easily overlook.

"Then God opened her eyes and she saw a well of water" Genesis 21:19

Moments before, Hagar, was blinded by fear and pain and could not see the well. Her own vision had been obscured by the grief in the present circumstance and uncertainty of the future. But in response to her son Ishmael's prayer (Genesis 21:17) God opened her eyes to see what was right in front of her all along. Sometimes fear can keep us from "seeing the forest for the trees", or pain can prevent us from recognizing our opportunity for healing, or discouragement can obscure our ability to perceive a provision in the midst of our lack. The solution to a problem may be right in front of you but in order to see it you may need your eyes refocused.

"Call to Me and I will answer you,
and I will tell you great and mighty things,
which you do not know.'
Jeremiah 33:3

There is a lot I can't see, don't understand, don't know about, and can't figure out, try as I might. But it is so comforting to know that when I can't see, He will be my eyes and help me to focus on where to take the next step, enabling me to recognize the opportunity.

Let's pray...
Father, I ask that you would open my eyes to see what I need to see. Give me Your vision and show me Your provision for my problem. Thank you that though Your ways are higher than mine, You mark out the path before me. In the glorious Name of Jesus! Amen!

Throughout the gospels we read how Jesus was moved with compassion. Over and over again Jesus demonstrated His compassion for people by stretching out His hand and touching the lives of others. Out of compassion He would move and bring healing. Out of compassion He would patiently teach, and out of that same compassion He would grant forgiveness, restoring hope to those beaten down by sin. He saw people with value and worth. He saw individuals who were created in the image of God and in need of Divine revelation and restoration.

In Luke chapter 7, Jesus patiently instructs Simon the Pharisee, while at the same time granting forgiveness to a repentant sinner. Here in the home of Simon, Jesus masterfully demonstrates and communicates the Fathers heart by asking one simple question...

"Simon, do you see this woman?"
Luke 7:44

This woman had been identified only as "a sinner". This was her identity! The reputation she had made for herself through a lifestyle of sin. Jesus could have said "Simon, do you see this sinner?" But instead Jesus wanted Simon to see her as a woman valued by God.

Simon knew about this woman. I am certain the whole town knew about this woman. But it is highly unlikely that he ever did anything out of compassion to help her. How can I be so certain? Because he was a Pharisee and their "MO" was to not even brush against common people, believing they would be defiled by the mere touch. Anyone with a reputation, like this woman had, would be kept at a safe distance. In fact, the Pharisee's had a saying "Let not a man associate with sinners even to bring them near the Torah". They had made a relationship with God and His word all about themselves, keeping it to themselves, and protecting themselves.

Yet, God's heart cries out for us to see beyond ourselves and look to the soul-needs of others, seeing their need for Divine revelation and restoration. He has chosen us to be the hands, feet, and voice to carry His message of love and redemption to a lost and hurting world. Whether they are a "Pharisee" (*the self-righteous),* or a "Sinner" (*the unrighteous),* the message of Christ is the cure for their condition. As disciples of Christ we must be willing to cross the man-made boundaries of prejudices, hate and judgment and do as Paul said:

"from now on, we regard no one
according to the flesh"
2 Corinthians 5:16

<u>Instead we must choose to look through the redemptive eyes of Christ!</u> Let's allow the compassion that moved Jesus to move us with redemptive words and loving actions.

Let's pray...
Father, I ask you to open my eyes to see those who are in need of the Savior's restoring touch today. Then please help me to step out in faith, knowing that You long to touch them with Your love. In the Name of my Lord and Savior Jesus! Amen!

"You were all called to travel on the same road and in the same direction, so stay together, both outwardly and inwardly. You have one Master, one faith, one baptism, one God and Father of all, who rules over all, works through all, and is present in all. Everything you are and think and do is permeated with Oneness."
Ephesians 4: 4-6 (The Message)

What is the largest living thing on earth? The Redwood tree! With an average height of over 300 feet these living giants are awe inspiring. Recently our ministry team was on an overnight planning retreat at Redwood Christian Park. While there we stood in the middle of a cluster of these amazing specimens, gazed upward and breathed in their heights.

Amazingly these trees actually have an extremely shallow root system. So what gives them the stability they need to reach their full potential? To grow to an average height of 360 feet without toppling over like a stilt left to stand on it's own? Their intertwining roots! Redwoods have a root system that extends over 100 feet wide and are interwoven with others in their growth cluster .

In a circle, we gathered grasping one another's hands, bowing our hearts and heads while praising God for our unity in Christ! We felt our hearts full of the wonder of God's design for us to accomplish together what we could never accomplish on our own.

To reach your full height and stature in Christ, to weather the storms, not be swept away by the floods or toppled by the winds of adversity, you need to have your roots interwoven with others that are heading the same direction: Upwards in Christ!

Let's pray...

Father, help me to extend my roots outward and interlink with other Christian women who have a heart for you, so together we can draw strength and support from one another. Thank you for your plan to set the lonely in Your family. In the Name of our One Lord, Jesus Christ! Amen!

Boldly Confident

"Now when they saw the boldness of Peter and John, and perceived that they were uneducated and untrained men, they marveled. And they realized that they had been with Jesus."
Acts 4:13

Now let's imagine if our names were in the place of Peter and John...
Now when they saw the boldness of _____ and *Lisa,*
and perceived that they were uneducated and untrained (women), they marveled. And they realized that they had been with Jesus.

If I am honest, sometimes "fear" and "timidity" can be a more fitting description than "boldness". Yet here we are given a description of two ordinary men in a difficult situation who displayed great courage. The word for "boldness" in Acts 4:13 is "parresia" and means: to speak openly or frankly. Peter and John were *confident* in what they were proclaiming, and therefore spoke with authority and boldness.

The world is in great need of Christians to walk in Christ-centered boldness. This passage gives us a key component of where that boldness comes from, "...they realized that they had been with Jesus". Quite simply, confidence comes from growing in our relationship with the Lord. The more we walk and talk with the Lord, and grow in the knowledge of His Word, His ways, and His heart the more confident we will be in sharing Him with others. Not forced but authentic!

Notice their boldness didn't come from specialized training and education ("they were uneducated and untrained men"). We are presently living in what is called the information age, and although there are great benefits to having information so readily available, it can also create a false sense of confidence. Many today are under the assumption that if "*I can only get a little more information*" about "*how to...*" somehow this will unlock the door to living a bolder, more confident life in Christ. This can become an endless pursuit of information and a substitute for walking in genuine faith and intimacy with the Lord. Yet, nothing can replace authentically encountering the nearness of God. True confidence comes from "*being with Jesus*"!

So along with those early disciples, let's draw near to Him and ask...

"*grant that your bondservants may speak your Word with all confidence*" (Acts 4:29)

Let's pray...
Father, as I draw near to you and spend time in the presence of Jesus please give me a holy impartation of bold confidence in sharing Your truth with others. May my motivation be love from a heart filled with the knowledge of You! In the Name that is above every name, Jesus Christ my Lord. Amen!

When I woke up this morning I began to think about my day before I was fully awake. There was laundry to do, dishes from last night, grocery shopping, phone calls, helping my husband with some paperwork and a number of other things I wanted to accomplish. As I considered what needed to be done and what I could do with the time left over, I suddenly became aware that I was making my choices for the day based on what *I* wanted to do rather than consulting the Lord about what He had on His heart for the day ahead. Each day we are given 24 hours in which there are certain things we must do like: sleep, eat, work, household and family responsibilities etc. Then there are certain things which we can choose to do with the hours left available like: reading, TV, exercising, hobbies, Facebook, phone calls and many other things. In both the "must do's" and the "choices" we are given tremendous opportunities.

"For we are His workmanship created
in Christ Jesus for good works,
which God prepared beforehand that
we should walk in them "
Ephesians 2:10

When I look at this passage the word "should" seems to leap off the page. I realize that just because God has strategically prepared "*good works*" for me to walk in doesn't guarantee I *will* walk in them. We are told here that we have been shaped, molded and prepared in Christ *to* walk in, engage in, and be occupied with "good works".

Every day, God in His loving-kindness, has prearranged opportunities for you and me to bring the presence of Christ into the world around us. Yet if I am too busy doing *my* own thing, making *my* own choices, preoccupied with *my* own to-do list I will miss most, if not all, of these opportunities. However, if I begin each day by first talking things over with Him, presenting my day to Him, allowing Him the opportunity to bring to mind some things I haven't considered, He will prepare my heart for the unfolding of the day. I will in turn have a more in-tune sense of His leading and a more Christ-centered, fruitful and productive day.

Let's pray...
Father help me to seek first Your Kingdom by seeking Your heart and mind as I begin each day. Get my heart in tune with Yours so that I can walk in the "good works" for which You have prepared me. In the sanctifying name of Jesus. Amen!

"...when I call to remembrance the genuine faith that is in you, which dwelt first in your grandmother Lois"
2 Timothy 1:5

I recently attended a memorial service where the grandson shared how a single phone call from his grandmother helped to pull him out of a dark and discouraging time. What did she say that made the difference? Was it something profound or deeply insightful? No, she simply shared how she was praying for him, loved him and was proud of him. Just a godly grandma expressing her faith in love.

Sometimes we fail to recognize the influence we have been given in Christ. Simple words spoken in faith and love carry the power to alter destinies! Grandma, your time has not passed- you are the matriarch of your family. Whether your family acknowledges it or not your words carry weight. What you speak into their lives will not soon be forgotten. A simple note, a phone call or a brief conversation can go a long way!

The young man who shared at the memorial service also stated that he and his grandma were not close. I know many grandmas whose hearts agonize over the lack of involvement they are granted in the lives of their grandchildren. Although nothing can make up for this sense of felt loss, it is encouraging to know that even the briefest of encounters can have a profound influence.

Grandma, remember who you are and make the most of your honored role. Your prayers, your words and your love are not sewn in vain. God has promised to make your descendants mighty on the earth! (Psalms 112:2) Declare it! Speak it! Pray it - Knowing that God watches over His word to perform it!

"The words that I speak to you are spirit, and they are life" John 6:63

Let's pray...
Father, thank you for grandchildren! May my prayers for them avail before You and may my words to them find a resting place in their hearts. As I proclaim Your Word over their life, I trust in Your mighty hand to bring it to pass. In the Name of Jesus. Amen!

"Draw me after you and let us run together!
The king has brought me into his chambers."
Song of Solomon 1:4 (NASB)

During the winter months, it is so inviting to curl up with a warm blanket and read a good, old-fashioned love story. One of my favorites is right out of the pages of scripture from Genesis 24. The story of Isaac and Rebekah. Rebekah is described as both beautiful and pure. Chosen to be loved, cherished and provided for by her husband-to-be. It truly is a beautiful romantic love story.

Ordained by God, since the foundation of the world, was the meeting of an unnamed servant and Rebekah by a well outside the city of Nahor. This servant, following the instructions of his master Abraham to seek out a wife for his son Isaac, traveled over 500 miles to find the land of his master's relatives in Mesopotamia. After traveling for many days he finally arrived one evening, stopping at the well outside the city. Since it was time for the women to come out and draw water the servant quickly asked the Lord for direction and clarity. He wanted to be certain that the woman to be chosen was chosen by the hand of God and not his own. Before he even finished his prayer the Lord had answered with Rebekah in an unmistakable way.

Rebekah had gone out that evening to draw water as she did every evening. In the course of her normal routine is where God filled the desire of this young girl's heart. Here, on her own door step, from five hundred miles away, without the internet, without chat rooms, without set-ups and "singles" groups, God worked out His good and perfect plan for the uniting of Isaac and Rebekah.

Upon the request and testimony of the servant, her family quickly acknowledged the hand of the Lord and gave their full approval. Gifts of gold, silver and fine garments were lavished on Rebekah and her family. These gifts assured that she would be well provided for through Isaac. Although the family desired Rebekah to delay in her departure, she made the decision to not put off the journey but make haste in beginning her new life with her soon-to-be husband, Isaac.

The last verse of Genesis 24 tells us...

"she became his wife, and he loved her"

My precious sisters, you are "Rebekah"! Pictured here in these passages as the beautiful bride of Christ. Through a pre-ordained appointment, God made His desire known, His desire for you to be brought to His Son. In response to your favorable *"Yes!"* He too presented a dowry, the promised Holy Spirit, guaranteeing the riches to come and pledging from that moment on to love you, to cherish you, to protect you, and provide for you. Joyfully taking full responsibility for your wellbeing! He ensured through the precious blood of our Savior that He could and would fully perform that which He had promised.

Just as Isaac loved Rebekah, the Lord loves you and appointed you to be His. He longs for you to grow in the knowledge and the depths of His great love, resting fully in the security of being His beloved.

Like Rebekah, who decided to quickly depart from her present way of life, making haste in drawing near to her groom, may we choose to turn away from all that holds us back and prevents us from enjoying the breadth of His intense love!

Let's pray...

Father, thank you for pursuing me, drawing me close to your heart, and lavishing me with your intense love. I joyfully choose You today and every day! As long as there is breath in my lungs I will choose You! "My Beloved is mine, and I am His." (SoS 2:16) In the Name of my Beloved, Jesus! Amen!

Cast your Burden

Woke up this morning and within a short time I could feel the burden of discouragement creeping in on me, like a virus trying to zap my strength and energy. A cloud seemed to settle over me like an early morning fog bank. My time with the Lord and fresh coffee didn't burn it off; it looked as though the sun would not shine through today. I wanted to complain to the Lord about my discouragement, but then I heard the still small voice of Holy Spirit say, "*cast it instead*".

When I think of casting something I think of casting a fishing line or casting a stone. It literally means to grab hold of something and throw it forcefully. Much more than showing, it's throwing! At times I can be guilty of show-and-tell prayers rather than a cast and throw prayer. You know, the kind where you tell God all about the problem, rehearsing and magnifying "it" rather than Him. This kind of prayer keeps the burden pinned to our shoulders rather than lobbing it onto His.

Cast your burden on the Lord,
And He shall sustain you;
He shall never permit the righteous to be moved.
Psalms 55:22

If we are truly going to cast our burdens, so that we can experience His sustaining joy-filled strength, two things are required. First we must identify the burden. What is actually causing the fear, pressure, or discouragement? Once it is honestly identified, then we can cast it. Secondly, we must commit to the cast. No half-hearted throws! No stopping mid-pitch. Throw and release! If we are deliberate and intentional, we will enter into true praise making a glorious exchange... His joy becomes our unshakable strength! *"He shall never permit the righteous to be moved* (defeated, cast down or shaken)"

Looks like the Son came through today after all!

Let's pray...
Father, sometimes I have sticky fingers. I hate the burden but I have difficulty truly releasing it to You. Today I give it all to You, placing it fully in Your trustworthy hands! When I am tempted to take it back remind me of this past tense transaction, this glorious exchange: my burden for Your peace! In the All-sufficient Name of Jesus! Amen!

Known by Name

"And when Jesus came to the place,
He looked up and saw him, and said to him,
"Zacchaeus, make haste and come down,
for today I must stay at your house.""
Luke 19:5

I love this encounter recorded for us in Luke between Jesus and Zacchaeus. Passing through Jericho Jesus takes notice of Zacchaeus. He calls to him by name, then highly honors this man of small stature by declaring openly he wants to stay at his house. Wow! It feels good to be noticed, called by name and honored! When it happens to us we feel greatly valued.

I have a dear friend who is an amazing example to me. Whenever someone approaches her (usually a homeless person) asking for "money" she always takes the time to slow down, look them in the eyes, and ask for their name. Then referring to them by name she asks for permission to pray a blessing over them, then graciously gives them whatever she feels led or able to do. She sets aside everything (prejudices, judgments, time, pride, fear) for the opportunity to affirm their value in the name of Jesus. She takes notice, calls them by name, and honors them with a special God-appointed blessing. She is a living demonstration of God's heart for the lost.

We all desperately need to know that God calls us by name, not by our sins! The more our heart is truly awakened to this, the freer we will be "to freely give what we have freely received".

The loving-kindness of the Lord is what leads people to look God-ward. Turning towards God is true repentance! Too often we are focused on turning people away from sin when our goal is to turn people to Jesus.

"So he (Zacchaeus) made haste and came down,
and received Him joyfully"
Luke 19:6.

Once we are turned toward Jesus and receive Him, His grace delivers and draws us away from our destructive sinful choices.

"Zacchaeus just stood there, a little stunned.
He stammered apologetically,
"Master, I give away half my income
to the poor-and if I'm caught cheating,
I pay four times the damages."

"Jesus said, "Today is salvation day in this home!
Here he is: Zacchaeus, son of Abraham!
For the Son of Man came
to find and restore the lost."
Luke 19:7-10 (The Message)

I can hear the joy-full, proud heart of Father God making this declaration! May we also hear Him clearly speak this over us so that He can also speak it through us!

_____, Daughter of Abraham! (Galatians 3:26)

Let's pray...

Father, I choose to walk in the truth of my new identity! Fill my heart with this reality, so that my life is a true reflection of who I now am in Christ and not who I was in my sin. To the glory of Jesus my Savior! Amen!

Newborn Hunger

"...like newborn babies,
long for the pure milk of the word,
so that by it you may grow in respect to salvation,
[3] if you have tasted the kindness of the Lord."
1 Peter 2:2-3 (NASB)

"...*like newborn babies-*" I believe no one can understand this verse better than a mother. That precious newborn babe comes out of the womb into the cold world, crying out every couple of hours not only for nourishment but also for nurturing. Cradled in close, hearing mommy's familiar heartbeat, feeling the warmth of her skin, and receiving the nutrients his tiny body craves, creates a very special time of bonding. I look back on those midnight feedings, with each of my three children, with special affection. Even though I was fatigued and tired, they are still some of my most cherished memories.

In the above passage, we are being instructed to "long for" or "desire" the Word of God like a newborn babe thirsting for its mother's milk. The Greek word used for "desire" (long for) in this text speaks of "intense yearning". Much like a newborn, each of us is in need of the nurturing and spiritual nutrients we receive from the special nearness of God and instruction of His Word. Yet, *unlike* a newborn babe this "intense yearning" isn't to be something we "out-grow," but rather we should become more aware of our need *as* we grow.

His nature is experienced in a profound way when we take time to draw near to Him through the instruction of His Word. Much like those intimate times of a mother nursing her babe, we are on the receiving end of His love and affection!

The result of a steady diet of feeding upon the pure, unpolluted Word of God is we grow up into all things in Christ. But our affinity for coming back again and again on a daily basis is directly linked to the end of this verse...

"if you have tasted the kindness of the Lord" (v3 NASB)

Getting hooked on His kindness! Not a *"have to"* but a *"want to"* is the primary motivation for our longing and desire to come close and feast upon His Word. We do it not fearing judgment or condemnation but in expectation of a Father's purifying, encouraging, compassionate love.

Let's pray...
Father, as I make a daily choice to come sit at Your feet and feed on Your Word, I ask that You would captivate my heart with Your lovingkindness. Stir up my hunger to know You and may this become the most treasured time of my everyday life! In the Name of Jesus, the Living Word! Amen!

A desolate Place

I have recently felt my heart being stirred by the Lord to respond to a particular need that is *way* beyond my abilities and resources. Maybe you can relate to having an excitement mixed with the sobering fear of a complete surrender. A heightened awareness to a particular need you can't seem to disconnect, mixed with a deep compassionate desire to respond. Yet all along you are aware that to the rational, natural mind it sounds absurd, because you have neither the ability nor the resources to accomplish the task. But in your heart and spirit, you know that it's the Lord nudging and guiding you into action.

In Matthew 14: 13-21...

It was getting late and the twelve apostles were acutely aware of the needs of this large multitude of people. Jesus had been tirelessly ministering to them all day and many had traveled far and were without food. Their tummies were grumbling and their bodies were aching. So the twelve disciples, with a measure of compassion, reasoned in their natural minds that the best solution for this enormous problem was to send the crowd away. They concluded: "we have nothing to offer"; "*we are in a desolate place*"(Luke 9:12).

When the Lord is preparing us to be of service in a mighty work, He often first opens our eyes and ears to make us keenly aware of a particular need and the *desolation* that surrounds the situation. It is after this awareness has seized us that His charge is usually given.

"Jesus said to them,... ' you give them something to eat'"(v16)

Mark's Gospel tells us they responded to Him by stating how much it would cost to feed the multitude "*two hundred denarii*" (equivalent to 6 months wages). Usually our first reaction to God's summons is "how much is it going to cost me?". To this the Lord responds, "*Bring Me what you have*" (v18). How much is it going to cost us? Everything! His call to us is to bring ALL that we have! He then will take what we bring and multiply it unto sufficiency.

"He took the five loaves and the two fish, and looking up to heaven, <u>He blessed and broke and gave the loaves to the disciples; and the disciples gave to the multitudes.</u>" (v19)

the result...

"<u>So they all ate and were filled,</u> and they took up twelve baskets full of the fragments that remained." (v20)

Wow!! Jesus provided everything they needed to serve the multitude and supplied enough for them as well. This is no magic trick. This is the God of the universe doing what He does best-making much of our little. So if, like me, you sense the Lord's prompting to step out and do what seems impossible, I encourage you to respond with your ALL so that He can supply ALL that is needed for the task through you.

For His glory and the furtherance of His Kingdom!

Let's pray...

Father, You know it can be oh so frightening to take a giant step of faith. Help me to remember I am not alone on this journey but I am partnered with You. And You have promised to supply all my needs according to Your glorious riches by Christ Jesus. In His Name I pray. Amen!

Chosen

For many years of my Christian life I felt like "the one" who had slipped in the back door. I wasn't raised in a Christian family like everyone around me *appeared* to be. I was a high school dropout and then a beauty school dropout! I was a former alcoholic and drug addict and had gotten pregnant at the age of 19 out of wedlock. I felt as if I had a giant "L" stamped on my forehead for "Loser". I reeked with underlying shame and a profound sense of inferiority even though I was, by the pure grace of God, saved and delivered at 20. This warped belief hindered my growth in Christ! Although I knew the Lord loved me, had forgiven me, and received me into His eternal family I reasoned, "*He kind of had to*, since He died for the sins of the world." I had no doubt I was loved by Him, but somehow I still felt like a second-class Christian, more of an afterthought. Slowly over the years, through the study of God's Word, I have become increasingly aware that He didn't love me because He *had to*, He loved me because He *wanted to*. There is a BIG difference between the two!

"... He chose us in Him before the foundation of the world, that we would be holy and blameless before Him. In love He predestined us to adoption as sons through Jesus Christ to Himself, according to the kind intention of His will"
Ephesians 1: 4-5

The above passage makes it abundantly clear- we are no afterthought. We've been chosen! Without allowing it to be sabotaged by the arguments that can surround this passage, I encourage you to simply let this affirming truth speak deeply into the inner recesses of your heart. God Almighty in eternity past, before He created any of the physical world, chose you in Christ! He set His eye and affections on you. He chose you not because He had to but because He wanted to! He chose you knowing all the bad decisions, all the wasteful living, all the rebellion, all the scars, wounds, and damage you would incur and would cause. With full knowledge, He chose you to be holy and blameless before Him. To not only redeem you but restore you to His original intentions for your life. He chose you in love to be loved by Him!

Wow!! How's that for esteem. Not self-esteem but God-esteem! (*Esteem*: to regard highly or favorably, to set a value on). This revelation has had a profound impact on my life!

Precious sister, I encourage you to ask the Lord to impress the reality of this upon your heart like never before. This is a liberating truth! It allows the presence of God to move more freely through you, restoring and helping you advance into all that He has in store for your life.

Let's pray...
Father, thank you for setting Your eye on me to redeem, restore and replenish my life with Your goodness. I choose to dwell in the security of Your great affirming love and the value You have placed upon my life. May all that You have dreamed for my life be my confident pursuit. For Your glory! In the name of Jesus, the Author of my salvation! Amen!

Faith and Destiny

I have seen some amazing doors of opportunity opened that no man could shut, but I have also known closed doors that were meant to be opened. There are many doors along our journey of life that will never be opened simply because we didn't pursue them by faith. But faith isn't just about what I believe it is also about what I do. A lesson to be learned from the life of Daniel!

"Then this Daniel began distinguishing himself among the commissioners and satraps because he possessed an <u>extraordinary spirit</u>, and the king planned to appoint him over the entire kingdom. Then the commissioners and satraps began trying to find a ground of accusation against Daniel in regard to government affairs; but they could find no ground of accusation or evidence of corruption, inasmuch as <u>he was faithful</u>, and <u>no negligence or corruption was to be found in him</u>."
Daniel 6: 3-4 (NASB)

These passages reveal three key areas that Daniel displayed <u>faith in action</u>:

- He possessed an extraordinary spirit (great attitude)
- He was faithful (diligent in his duties)

- He was without corruption (integrity of character)

The governors in the passage above were consumed with jealousy. Seemingly they succeeded in their plot by having Daniel thrown into a lion's den. But this proved to be only temporary because a day later their plot backfired when they ended up in the lion's den themselves. (See Daniel 6)

Plots, schemes, false accusations, a string of "bad luck", not even a den of hungry lions could prevent Daniel from coming into the destiny God had for him. But there was one thing that could have hindered him from fulfilling his purpose: FAITH. His faith needed to be lived out in the day-to-day activities of life.

<u>Faith in action is the only thing between us and our destiny!</u>

Don't allow the enemy to steal your destiny by living a life of mediocrity, faithlessness, murmuring and/or compromise. Instead, choose to live today aboveboard by trusting God and demonstrating your faith through your actions! This plays an important role in opening doors of divine destiny in your life while at the same time shutting the mouths of lions.

"So Daniel was taken up out of the den
and no injury whatever was found on him,
because he had trusted in his God."
Daniel 6:23 (NASB)

Let's pray...
Father, may I be found faithful in all my ways as I lean into You and rely on Holy Spirit's overcoming presence in my day-to-day life. I declare that no weapon formed against me will prosper, because this is my heritage as Your daughter! In the faithful, overcoming Name of Jesus, Amen!

Intense Desire

There are times when the Holy Spirit arrests my heart with a particular verse and draws me in to further discovery. This following verse contains a majestic jewel worth some serious pondering. What the Lord revealed to me, and I will now *attempt* to share with you, has brought me to a renewed sense of awe-struck wonder of His amazing love! In this familiar passage Jesus has just sat down to intimately share a Passover meal with His disciples. It is there that the Lord shares these words right from His heart...

> *" And He said to them,*
> *"I have earnestly desired to eat*
> *this Passover with you before I suffer;"*
> *Luke 22:15 (NASB)*

This Passover meal was distinctly different from all others. He had shared at least one and possibly two other Passover's with these soon to be apostles, *but* He makes a clear distinction regarding this Passover celebration through the words "before I suffer." This particular Passover was extremely special because it would inaugurate the New Covenant relationship His "suffering" would secure.

Although the Passover and the new covenant are worth in-depth consideration, it was the words "earnestly desired" that captured my attention and my heart. In the original Greek two words for desire are placed together here to emphasize the strongest form of desire conceivable.

With the full weight of the cross in view, Jesus expresses that He had longed with "intense desire" for this moment in history. The question is; *how long*? How long had He desired for this particular night and occasion to come? Was it since the previous Passover? Or since He was baptized and officially began His earthly ministry? Could He possibly be referring to a time even before His earthly ministry? Perhaps His longing began when He first spoke to the prophet Jeremiah about the coming of a new covenant, ushering in a new relationship. It might have been when His glory filled the Temple the day it was consecrated, looking toward the day when His glory would fill our hearts. Maybe it was long before, when He instituted the first Passover delivering Israel from the Iron Furnace, keeping this special one in His steadfast gaze. Possibly it was even longer ago when He spoke to Abraham to initiate His covenant and declared that all the nations of the earth would be blessed through Abraham's Seed.

Or maybe... Although it is true that this intense longing has been present in God's heart throughout ALL of redemptive history, it is also true that it *began* the moment a great rending occurred in the Garden of Eden. When Adam and Eve made their willful decision to oppose God. That moment of separation from *His* beloved, crown of creation, brought an intense longing with an intense desire to usher in the rending of the veil of sin that kept us from intimate fellowship with Himself. Precious sister, since time began God has set His heart, affection, purposes, and intention on restoring you to the position for which you were created: everlasting closeness, intimacy and fellowship with Himself.

YOU *are* His "intense desire"!
This is a love worth celebrating! Mission accomplished through Christ! Let's breathe it in and live in its fullness until we see Him face to face and celebrate with Him in His kingdom, where the fullness of His desire will be realized!!!!!

Let's pray...

Father, your intense love amazes me! I am so thankful for ALL you have done to make it possible for me to spend eternity with You and to never again be separated from Your love! Today I celebrate Your indescribable gift in Jesus with renewed awe and wonder. In the saving Name of Jesus. Amen!

"I cannot find peace, or remember happiness. I tell myself, "I am finished! I can't count on the Lord to do anything for me. Just thinking of my troubles and my lonely wandering   makes me miserable. That's all I ever think about, and I am depressed."
Lamentations 3:17-20 (ESV)

Can you relate? Have you ever felt so emotionally fatigued and trapped by the weight of your circumstances that you thought "I am finished!" Maybe you have been calling out to God but you see no relief or change in sight. You desperately want peace but it seems to evade you. Does it feel as if you are locked-in and someone has thrown away the key to your relief?

Frustration! - Anger! - Despair!

The truth is we are all vulnerable to discouragement and depression. After preaching and prophesying for 40 years, Jeremiah watched his fellow Israelites get taken away into captivity. He gave it his very best and they refused to listen. Now his heart was in anguish over what felt like complete failure and hopelessness. All he could see was trouble and misery.

So, what is the answer? How do we move from victim to victory? How does a downcast, weary soul get renewed with hope and strength? What is the key that unlocks the prison of despair?

Jeremiah shows us the answer in the next passage. <u>Read it through and notice the progression.</u>

"This I recall to my mind, Therefore I have hope.
The Lord's lovingkindnesses indeed never cease,
For His compassions never fail.
They are new every morning;
Great is Your faithfulness."

"The Lord is my portion," says my soul,
<u>*"Therefore I have hope in Him."*</u>
Lamentations 3:21-24 (NASB)

Jeremiah remembers the nature of His great and all-powerful God. He changes his focus from rehearsing the trouble to proclaiming the unchanging faithfulness of God. Many times, we are caught in a cycle of despair because our troubles are *"all we ever think about"* v20. When we make a decision to turn our attention, thoughts and meditation on the Lord, faith is activated and hope restored. This is why *"faith is the substance of things hoped for, the evidence of things not seen"* Hebrews 11:1

Downcast to an up-cast!

Let's pray...
Father, give me a renewed glimpse of your glory that produces an intimate knowledge that with You nothing shall be impossible! Great is Your faithfulness - therefore I have hope! In Jesus name! Amen.

Ordinary to Extraordinary

"He has no form or comeliness,
and when we see Him there is
no beauty that we should desire Him.
He is despised and rejected by men,
a Man of sorrows and acquainted with grief
and we hid as it were our faces from Him."
Isaiah 53:2b-3

This description reveals an important reality behind the successful ministry of Jesus. Jesus wasn't a showman practicing showmanship! He didn't have a pleasing appearance or a dynamic personality that drew people to Him, as is often the case with so many highly-esteemed and sought-after individuals in the world. Prior to His public ministry He wasn't the person people would look at, observe, and hold up as someone they would aspire to become. He isn't the guy who would have been chosen as prom king in high school, He wouldn't have been voted most likely to succeed. He didn't wear designer clothes, attend the best schools, or have the right kind of connections. All the things that we would normally consider necessary for success were not part of His lot in life. For 30 years Jesus lived a very ordinary life among a disadvantaged, impoverished people, working by the sweat of His brow.

Then at the age of 30 something catapulted Him from a life of obscurity to becoming a public figure who accomplished a great work.

What made the difference?

Did He inherit a large chunk of money? Did He finally get His big break, being recognized for His great skills and talent? Did He meet the "right" people and come into the "right" crowd? Of course the answer is No, No, and No! A dynamic shift took place when Jesus was baptized by the Spirt of God. Remember Jesus was born without a sin nature, so He always had the Spirit within Him, He always had fellowship with God, and He always loved people. But the power of the Holy Spirit coming upon Him made it possible for Him (in His human nature) to love people beyond a mere human capacity, bringing hope and restoration to lives that were broken and disabled by the curse and sin.

People sought Him out because He preached a message that revealed the heart of God, the good news of the Kingdom of God, and was authenticated by the power of God. People hungered for reality, not religion, "for He taught them as one having authority, and not as the scribes." (Matthew 7:29) The same is true today; people are hungry to see, hear, and taste the reality of God, not religion or something manufactured through human efforts. Jesus has made it possible for us to also receive the "promise" of the Holy Spirit, so that we can continue to effectively and successfully preach the Good News of His Kingdom.

The centerpiece that should be on display, the thing that will draw in the thirsty, the broken, downcast, empty, hurting, Truth-seekers is Jesus Christ being presented in the power of the Spirit! Although there is nothing wrong with using what is available to proclaim Him and His message, we must do so without veiling or substituting His strength and beauty.

"Whoever speaks on their own
does so to gain personal glory,
but he who seeks the glory of the one who sent him

is a man of truth;
there is nothing false about him."
John 7:18

The Holy Spirit who makes us coheirs with Christ can take your ordinary life and accomplish extraordinary things if you will allow him to do so and lay aside the less sufficient means of human effort. Ask Him to fill you afresh today and mark you with His authenticity!

Let's pray...
Father, praise Your name for the gift of my salvation and the promise of the Holy Spirit. I ask to be filled to overflowing today and that You would mark my life with the glorious fruit of Your nature. May the fragrance of Christ be authentic and powerful in me and through me. In Jesus Name, Amen!

Waiting and Wondering

Waiting on the Lord? Praying? Things seem to be getting worse not better? Wondering what God is doing? Feeling discouraged? You are not alone it happens to all of us! But keep in mind, some of the Lord's best work progresses in seemingly detrimental ways.

Here is an example:

"The Lord hardened Pharaoh's heart, and he did not let the children of Israel go"
Exodus 11:10

Interesting... God hardened, NOT softened!
He used the unexpected to bring His ultimate deliverance.
<u>Things got worse before they got better.</u>

Does deliverance seem delayed?

Remember this...

"When he lets you go, he will surely drive you out of here <u>altogether</u>"
Exodus 11:1

God was not aiming for a partial or temporary freedom. His work is thorough!

Don't short circuit the process or settle for less than His good and perfect goal. He is seeking to accomplish something authentic and complete!

Finally...

"and it shall be, when you go, you shall not go empty handed"
Exodus 3:21b

When the deliverance comes, when the victory is realized, you can be certain He will do more than just deliver, He will bring you out full!

That is just the kind of God He is and the way He operates. Expect nothing less!

Let's pray...
Father, as I wait for my breakthrough help me to meditate on your goal not the present problem. Your wisdom, grace, and Word will be my food. May Your glorious will be thoroughly accomplished! In the name of Jesus my strong Deliverer! Amen!

Living a Legacy

Among my top five favorite biographies is, "The Life of *George Mueller*"! *This* amazing man lived in the 1800's and was known for his work of faith among the orphans. I recently read that when he began the work to house orphans in 1834 there were only enough accommodations, throughout all of England combined, for 3,600 orphaned children. But just fifty years later his work had so inspired the people of England that over 100,000 orphans were being cared for and housed. In his lifetime 10,000 orphans were provided for through his own partnership with the Lord. But his <u>living example</u> revolutionized the plight of orphans in England far beyond his own personal involvement.

For most of us our example of faith will be what bears the greatest fruit, going far beyond what we say and do at a point in time, in a given situation. Maybe you have wondered if your "day to day" faith really matters that much. Let me just respond by saying "YES, it does!!" Much more than you realize.

"Let your light shine before men
in such a way that they may see your good works,
and glorify your Father who is in heaven."
Matthew 5:16

The Lord desires for us to live in a way that will inspire others toward greater degrees of faith. When we make daily choices to trust the Lord when times are good and everything seems to be "coming up roses" as well as when things are *not so good* or downright painful, we are communicating to those around us God can be trusted with the realities of life.

> **"But sanctify the Lord God in your hearts,**
> **and always be ready to give a defense**
> **to everyone that asks you**
> **the reason for the hope that is in you"**
> **1 Peter 3:15**

As a pastor George Mueller set out to establish a house for orphans to demonstrate that God could be fully depended upon. The ministry faced every challenge possible while fully relying upon the Lord. He wanted to provide a living illustration of God's faithfulness. The illustration grew far beyond what he had thought or imagined. This man's life was truly a living epistle that is still speaking today.

Your life is a living sermon!
Let it preach His faithfulness!
Pray in faith, stand in faith, walk in faith and yes... run in faith too! Let God be found true in everything you do! The result will be: a living testimony that speaks beyond the grave!

Let's pray...
Father, You ARE faithful! Let this be the truth that defines my life day by day. I choose to trust You, hope in You, rejoice in You, walk with You, and praise You with my life today. In the Name of Jesus-the Way the Truth and the Life! Amen

"Act as if what you do makes a difference. It does!" - William James

Why Persevere?

Have you ever done something good only to be rewarded with evil? Fought for justice only to see injustice prevail? It can be frustrating, heartbreaking, discouraging and even feel downright oppressive! It is here, in that place of what looks like defeat, we can feel like giving up. We can be inclined to think, "Why bother?".

"Let us not lose heart in doing good,
for in due time we will reap
if we do not grow weary."
Galatians 6:9 (NASB)

We need, in times like these, to be very deliberate about "putting on the mind of Christ". The above passage (Galatians 6:9) promises that there will be a day of reaping "if" we do not grow weary. Other translations say "if we do not give up". Jesus Christ is our beaming example of God's ability to take a bad, unfair, unjust, and even horrific circumstance and bring about something good and glorious. The most tragic, unjust, horrific event since the world began was Jesus the spotless Son of God crucified. Yet His crucifixion was also the greatest triumph and blessing ever accomplished for mankind!

<u>When things look the darkest, remember the cross!</u>

Because of what Jesus did on that cross, the same hope and triumph is promised to us who persevere by grace in faith.

"He who did not spare His own Son,
but delivered Him up for us all,
how shall He not with Him
also freely give us all things?"
Romans 8:32

The answer is YES, He will!

Hang on tight and watch the God of wonders work His miracles through your circumstance. The victory has already been secured and now your faith will usher it in.

Let's pray...
Father, help me to see the victory of Christ over the enemy and to not give up in the darkest hour. Fill me with faith and strength to persevere until I see ALL things put under your feet! In the name of Jesus, the Captain of my salvation! Amen!

"You shall also be a crown of glory In the hand of the Lord, And a royal diadem In the hand of your God."
Isaiah 62:3

Here is the power, the power of God to transform a life and make it something of incredible beauty and brilliance. A masterpiece in the making, fashioned for display! Much like the forming of a diamond...

Did you know that a diamond is a gemstone that represents steadfast love? It's considered to be one of the most beautiful gemstones in the whole world. It's Greek name is "adamas" meaning 'unbreakable' or 'indestructible'. A stone that is meant for eternity! Yet in order for a diamond to truly be magnificent and durable, it must first go through a tremendous amount of heat and pressure. Once it has been formed, for it to have significant value, it must be cut by an expert cutter with absolute precision. Finally, for its beauty to be displayed it needs light, light that is both received and diffused.

This is His aim, His purpose, His destiny for each of us who are in Christ. Through the intimate work of His hands and the strategic purpose of His plans to shape us into something spectacular for all eternity, through which His glory can shine!

The key, however, is being in the hand of the Lord, remaining in the hand of our God as He continues to fashion us. When the pressure is extended over a period of time, our tendency can be to look for an escape hatch, a way out! Yet if we will remember His purpose is not for our harm but for our greatest good, His grace will abound toward us. Then the beautification process can continue forming us into a precious jewel, a crown of glory.

Let's pray...
Father, help me to rest in your hand of love. I want to see through eyes of faith and value what You are accomplishing. I choose to cooperate and not resist but stay in a trusting, yielded position as you continue to form me into a Masterpiece for Your glory. In the Name of Jesus, the Lord of Glory-Amen!

"*Therefore we do not lose heart. Even though our outward man is perishing, yet the inward man is being renewed day by day*" 2 Corinthians 4:16

Promised Purpose

My family has a Christmas tradition of watching, "It's A Wonderful Life". Even though I have watched this movie every Christmas for over 25 years, I still get teary eyed when Mr. Potter tells George Bailey he is worth more dead than alive. And of course I cry tears of joy at the end, when the Angel Clarence has successfully shown George what a tremendous impact his life has had for good on so many people. There is something deep within each of us that longs to know our life is making a difference.

In John 15: 16 Jesus speaking to His disciples says...

"You did not choose Me but I chose you, and appointed you that you would go and bear fruit and that your fruit would remain so that whatever you ask of the Father in My name He may give to you." John 15:16

This particular verse thrills me to no end! Or as my kids would say "It causes me to be *stoked.*" (*stoke*: to tend the fire of a furnace; to supply with fuel) Yes, that is the correct word to use here. As a disciple of Jesus Christ I want to know, *I need to know*, that my life is making a difference. That I am doing what I am supposed to do and bearing fruit doing it! The word "appointed" in this particular verse has to do with placement as well as potential. Each of us has been given a very specific assignment and placement in the world. The Lord has endued each of us with the precise gifts needed to walk-out or live-out the unique assignment He has chosen for us to accomplish. When we do what He has ordained for us, the result will be "fruit that remains". Purpose that makes a lasting difference! The Message bible reads this way:

"You didn't choose me, remember;
I chose you, and put you in the world to bear
fruit, fruit that won't spoil.
As fruit bearers, whatever you ask the Father in
relation to me, he gives you."
John 15:16 (The Message)

Did you catch the last part of this verse? A powerful promise for us is given here to accomplish the purpose we have been sent to do. The enemy will try to derail you, distract you, discourage you, afflict you, oppress you, and whatever else he can do to take you away from that good work. But God has promised that, as we are living out what He has ordained us for, we can call upon Him to receive whatever we need to continue forward with the work. God has ordained you, gifted you and availed all the resources of heavens power to assure your success! Don't allow the threats of the enemy to hinder your progress, but rather go forth with confidence and boldness in the Lord. Praising God for the victory Jesus has secured!

Let's pray...

Father, I long for every day of my life to be fruitful. Thank you for giving me a glorious purpose! I acknowledge that in Christ everything I need for life and godliness has been granted to me. In Him is a consistent "yes" to Your promises, to which I give my hearty Amen (or let it be so)! In the mighty Name of Jesus, Amen!

As He Is

"...We know that when He appears,
we will be like Him,
because we will see Him
just as He is."
1 John 3:2

<u>Seeing Christ "*as He is*" transforms who we are!</u>

Recently I was at a grocery store in the check out line when quite a commotion occurred over a homeless man standing out front. I had taken notice of this man when I walked in because he stood out like an Eskimo at the beach. He was covered in filth from head to toe, was carrying his bedding, and his hair was so matted it looked like he hadn't groomed himself in a couple years. I didn't give him too much thought till the cashier on my way out mentioned a ruckus that was created when they apparently asked "the homeless man" to leave. Her remarks were somewhat derogatory. When I left I felt a sense of grief. Not because of the cashier's remarks but because of my own insensitivity.

I had noticed him, but only from a physical human perspective, then moved on without a second thought. I sensed the Lord impressing on my heart that *He saw* the man behind the mess, and when I take notice of people I need to move beyond the human perspective and seek to see them with His eyes through the Spirit.

<u>I believe this is a BIG part of being conformed to the image of Christ.</u>

Bringing Him into everything allows me to see Him "*as He is*". To see Him as compassionate, to see Him full of grace and truth, to see Him as the Savior, as Shepherd, as Lord, Redeemer, Wonderful Counselor, to see Him as God!

> **"And do not be conformed to this world,**
> **but be transformed by**
> **the renewing of your mind,..."**
> **Romans 12:2**

Being transformed requires a conscience, deliberate effort of putting on the mind of Christ. This happens as I feed on His Word and acknowledge His presence, dialoguing with Him through the details and occurrences of everyday life.

Praying I see Him more and more "*as He is*"!

Let's pray...
Father, my heart longs to see Jesus for who He is. Please open the eyes of my heart to more revelation of the beauty of Christ. As I behold Him I pray I will become like Him! In the Name of the One who perfectly revealed Your heart, Jesus. Amen!

Joshua's Secret

" All the people saw the pillar of cloud standing at the tabernacle door, and all the people rose and worshiped, each man in his tent door. So the Lord spoke to Moses face to face, as a man speaks to his friend. And he would return to the camp, but his servant Joshua the son of Nun, a young man, did not depart from the tabernacle."
Exodus 33:8-10

These passages reveal Joshua's secret for a flourishing faith in the midst of those who had a failure of faith when the hour of testing came.

Here God pulls back the curtain for us to see what prepared Joshua to have a faith-fueled response when spying out the "promised land" (Numbers 14:6-9). Joshua, like us, wasn't naturally inclined to respond with faith. It wasn't like he simply had a cheery disposition or was more prone to having a positive outlook, seeing the cup half full.

Joshua, who was a servant of Moses, had a full plate of responsibilities. However, when he had free time he made it a priority to be in the presence of the Lord, gazing at the beauty of the Lord and being instructed in the ways of the Lord. When the hour of testing came, Joshua responded out of the reservoir that had been stored up within his heart.

All those who were content with worshipping *at a distance* didn't want to put out the effort to seek the Lord. So in the hour of difficulty, their time of testing, they too responded from what they had stored up, and it proved to be shallow. These are the same ones who perished in the wilderness, never entering or possessing the "promised land."

What we choose to do on a daily basis prepares us for the "greater" things God has in store- those faith challenges that will take us into our "promised land." Make the most of today by choosing to spend valuable alone time with the Lord in his word, bringing your heart fully into His Presence.

Let's pray...
Father, help me to be faithful in meeting with You like Joshua did, allowing You to speak into my life daily, so when the time comes for testing I will lay hold of all that You have purposed for me! In The name that is worthy to be praised, Jesus Christ, Amen!

"Having a positive outlook on life is not the power of positive thinking it's the companion of God-centered thinking." Louie Giglio

Prepared and Ready

Not that long ago our landlord did home inspections on all the properties she owns. She gave us the date a couple months out so that we would have an ample amount of time to prepare. Although I try to keep the house we rent fairly clean and orderly, it definitely motivated me to take care of some of the little extras I never seem to get around to doing. With the goal in mind, I planned and purposed to make the most of this opportunity. It felt good to clear out some of the extra clutter and clean some areas that often get overlooked. When all was said and done, she thanked us for taking good care of her house and treating it like a home. As a result of this extra effort, I felt prepared to welcome any unexpected visitors into our home with confidence. All the rooms fit for a kingly visit.

This reminds me of an exhortation given by Paul in 2 Timothy...

"But in a great house there are not only vessels of gold and silver, but also of wood and clay, some for honor and some for dishonor. Therefore if anyone cleanses himself from the latter, he will be a vessel for honor, sanctified and useful for the Master, prepared for every good work." 2 Timothy 2:20-21

My heart longs to be useful to the Master, and this experience reminded me how important it is to stay prepared. I sometimes go through what feels like a dry-spell. Not much seems to be moving and shaking. But it is during these times I need to not only <u>be</u> prepared but <u>stay</u> prepared for the next opportunity. It is entirely at God's discretion when and how He will put a vessel into service. It is my responsibility to be prepared and ready. Yet unless we know what we are preparing for, it is difficult to be motivated and disciplined. It can be like preparing to run a race without knowing when, where or how long the race will be. But the Lord has not left us clueless. The Holy Spirit knows exactly what, when and where. If we are willing to listen He will clue us in on things to come.

"However, when He, the Spirit of truth, has come... ... He will tell you things to come." John 16:13a,b

<u>The motivation for how I live today comes from knowing the plans God has for my destiny.</u> If you haven't already, I encourage you to allow God to fuel your heart with a fresh vision for your future and the good works waiting for you to walk into, fully prepared and equipped. Keeping this vision in front of you will help to keep you motivated, living intentionally each day to prepare for and connect with the Master's "calling".

"Blessed are those servants whom the master, when he comes, will find watching." Luke 12:37

Let's pray...
Father, I want to be a prepared vessel ready to be put to use whenever You call. I pray Holy Spirit that You would keep my heart fueled with fresh vision for the future, while helping me to fully engage with Your plans for this day. In the blessed Name of Jesus. Amen!

At the age of seventy, George Mueller began to make great evangelistic tours. He traveled 200,000 miles, going around the world and preaching in many lands and in several different languages. He frequently spoke to as many as 4,500 or 5,000 persons. Three times he preached throughout the length and breadth of the United States. He continued his missionary or evangelistic tours *until he was ninety years of age*. He estimated that during these seventeen years of evangelistic work he addressed three million people. All his expenses were sent in answer to the prayer of faith." (Quote taken from ochristian.com)

Do you ever feel as though opportunity has passed you by? Like it's too late for a dream to be realized? That you are too old to accomplish anything of significance? Our culture tends to communicate that youth is the optimal time for success, and beyond a certain point you shouldn't expect much. But what may be impossible for man is certainly not impossible with God. He often reserves the best for last! Sarah became a mom at 90, the Apostle John wrote the book of Revelation very late in life and Moses led the Israelites out of Egypt at 80 years of age. My personal favorite is Caleb...

"...and now, here I am this day, eighty-five years old. As yet I am as strong this day as on the day that Moses sent me; just as my strength was then, so now is my strength for war, both for going out and for coming in. Now therefore, give me this mountain of which the Lord spoke in that day; for you heard in that day how the Anakim were there, and that the cities were great and fortified. It may be that the Lord will be with me, and I shall be able to drive them out as the Lord said."
"...Hebron therefore became the inheritance of Caleb the son of Jephunneh the Kenizzite to this day, because he wholly followed the Lord God of Israel."
Joshua 14:12-14

In all of these the key was faith in God, not looking to their own strength, ability or resources.

Our God leads us from glory to glory, *not* glory to insignificance. As a Christian our days ahead are always meant to be better than our days gone by, as we learn to walk more and more in the benefits of His lovingkindness. The voice of God speaks beauty and significance over our future. Any other message is not the voice of God! So if you find yourself in a slump thinking, "I am getting older...", drink in the following promise...

"Bless the Lord, O my soul;
And forget not all His benefits;
Who forgives all your iniquities,
Who heals all your diseases,

Who redeems your life from destruction,
Who crowns you with
lovingkindness and tender mercies,
Who satisfies your mouth with good things,
so that your youth is renewed like the eagle's. "
Psalms 103:2-5

Then let God renew your vision for a glorious future!

Let's pray...

Father, it is good to be Yours! You make all things beautiful and I acknowledge Your plans for my future are full of Your goodness, satisfying beyond compare. Renew my strength in the days to come so I can soar for Your glory. In the Mighty, life-giving Name of Jesus. Amen!

"For with God nothing will be impossible"
Luke 1:37

The first time these words were spoken in the gospels were through an angel speaking directly to Mary. Thirty years later Jesus would speak the same message using similar words to His own disciples. But my thoughts today are drawn to Mary. I wonder how many times she spoke and by faith anchored herself to these courage-infusing words? No doubt this truth was deeply etched upon her heart and soul through the storms of life.

<u>Each time she faced a seemingly impossible challenge her declaration became...</u>

"with God nothing will be impossible!!"

When she told her family and Joseph she was pregnant and the fear of being stoned or ostracized from her community loomed over her...

"with God nothing will be impossible!"

When late in pregnancy she had to travel a great distance and face giving birth far away from the support of her family...

"with God nothing will be impossible!"

When the only place available to give birth was in a dark, dank cave she faced it bravely knowing...

"with God nothing will be impossible!"

When she held baby Jesus in her arms for the first time and wondered how she could ever be the kind of mother the Messiah needed, she remembered...

"with God nothing will be impossible!"

When fleeing to Egypt with a newborn baby, not knowing where they would stay or how they would live, she trusted...

"with God nothing will be impossible!"

When as a family they faced times of leanness in harsh conditions not knowing if there would be enough food, she believed...

"with God nothing will be impossible!"

*When she lost her husband and had to go forward as a single mom...

"with God nothing will be impossible!"

When she watched the brutal world crucify her firstborn Son, the Promised One, she held tightly to...

"With God nothing will be impossible!"

When she heard and saw "He has risen" she REJOICED...

"WITH GOD NOTHING WILL BE IMPOSSIBLE!!"

What are you facing this season? Let this be your tag line! Anchor yourself to it by declaring it with confidence over the circumstance you face...

"with God nothing will be impossible!"

Let's pray...

Father, I declare <u>with You</u> *nothing will be impossible! Let this be stamped to the inside of my eyelids so that it is how I begin and end each day. May it define how I face every challenge, and may I grow all the more confident as it is proved over and over in my life. Praise the glorious Name of Jesus. Amen!*

*Most commentators believe Joseph passed away some time before Jesus began His ministry, since he is not mentioned.

Lisa Cook

About the Author

Lisa Cook is helping women to discover and live in the fullness of God's great love through Christ! She considers it to be one of her greatest privileges and passions to teach the Word of God and has done so faithfully for nearly twenty years. Lisa is the featured speaker and a co-founder of 4 His Beloved radio ministry and events. This ministry was birthed out of a desire to see women know the riches of Christ and the depths of His love.
You can find out more about Lisa Cook and 4 His Beloved Ministries at:

www.4HisBeloved.org

You can also connect with Lisa and the Ministry on:
Facebook/ 4hisbeloved
Twitter @4hisbeloved

A note from Lisa

Hello, Precious Sister!

My desire and continual prayer is to dive into the deep end of God's love! As I do I want to take you with me to discover the riches to be mined in the depths of His Word.

"I am my Beloved's and He is mine" is the romance He desires our life to be shaped through and known for. Will you join me and hundreds of other women who have made the decision with us to be head over heels in love with Him?

I encourage you to stop by our little spot on the web and connect with us by signing up for free inspiring devotional nuggets sent by email or **listen to free messages available weekly** through the radio ministry. If you sign up for emails you will also be notified about upcoming 4 His Beloved conferences and events that are bringing women into freedom, fullness, purpose and the abundant promises of being in Christ!

Would love the opportunity to connect with you face-to-face at an event! So be sure to sign up at

www.4HisBeloved.org

About "4 His Beloved Ministries"

4 His Beloved is a non-profit ministry to women focused on connecting the heart of women with the heart of God

Since 2010 we have been holding events for women of all ages at various churches and facilities. Women gather together from a variety of different churches, fellowships and denominations to experience the life-changing Presence of God through Worship and the Word.

In 2013, we added "4 His Beloved" radio ministry. Lisa Cook is the host and bible teacher for this weekly program for women. This broadcast airs weekly on several stations throughout the United States

Our God-given assignment is to equip women to live passionately and effectively for the kingdom of God by helping them to grow in freedom, fullness, purpose and potential through the power of Christ, His life-transforming Word, and His Glorious Presence.

We want to see a bible-based, Spirit-filled renewal spread abroad in the hearts of God's daughters. Igniting a generation of women to live passionately and confidently for His Glory!

For additional products and study tools be sure to visit: www.4HisBeloved.org

AUDIO DOWNLOAD

Discover
the glory of
the
New Covenant

8 Teachings

Discover the *Riches*
of your inheritance

"I am my Beloved's and He is mine"

Our Cherished Bond

Our Cherished Bond
Lisa Cook

The
Redemptive Names
of our
Redeeming God!

Download a FREE
Study Guide

@ www.4HisBeloved.org

Made in the USA
Las Vegas, NV
06 June 2021

24314005R00046